To: _____

From: _____

Date: _____

Blessed is the influence of one true, loving human soul on another.

George Eliot

Sweet Treats for My Friend

Artwork by Lisa Kaus

H

HARVEST HOUSE PUBLISHERS

EUGENE, OREGON

Sweet Treats for My Friend

Artwork copyright © 2012 by Lisa Kaus

Published by Harvest House Publishers
Eugene, Oregon 97402
www.harvesthousepublishers.com

ISBN 978-0-7369-4609-4

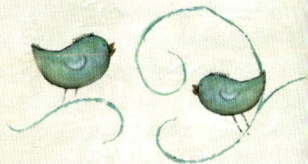

Design and production by Mary pat Design, Westport, Connecticut

Harvest House Publishers has made every effort to trace the ownership of all poems and quotes. In the event of a question arising from the use of a poem or quote, we regret any error made and will be pleased to make the necessary correction in future editions of this book.

All Scripture quotations, unless otherwise indicated, are taken from The Holy Bible, *New International Version*® *NIV*®. Copyright © 1973, 1978, 1984, 2011 by Biblica, Inc.™ Used by permission. All rights reserved worldwide.

Printed in China

12 13 14 15 16 17 / LP / 10 9 8 7 6 5 4 3 2 1

Friends…they cherish each other's hopes. They are kind to each other's dreams.

Henry David Thoreau

EAT CAKE

Be blessed.

Life is to be fortified by many friendships. To love and be loved is the greatest happiness of existence.

Sydney Smith

*There is nothing better than a friend,
unless it is a friend with chocolate.*

Charles Dickens

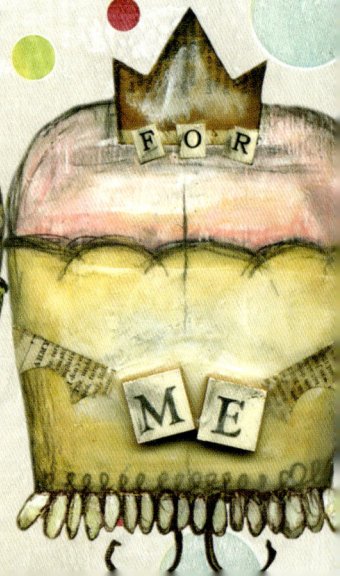

Make
a
WISH

FOR
ME

White Hot Chocolate

- 1¼ cups 1% low-fat milk
- ⅓ cup white chocolate
- ¼ teaspoon cinnamon
- ⅛ teaspoon nutmeg
- ¼ teaspoon real vanilla extract

Pour half of milk into a small pan. Add other ingredients. Stir often while heating mixture on medium heat to almost boiling. Add remaining milk and stir well. Remove from heat. Serve in mugs with a dusting of cinnamon and fine dark chocolate shavings.

You flavor my world with joy!

Sweet treats to top off a good day:

- ❖ a late night tête-à-tête
- ❖ ice-cream sundaes
- ❖ a midnight movie

SWEET TREATS TO SHARE:
- ❖ a bike ride
- ❖ a long walk
- ❖ a warm, sunny beach

Who finds a faithful friend, finds a treasure.

Jewish Proverb

We must eat cake... every day!

Many kinds of fruit grow upon the tree of life, but none so sweet as friendship.

Lucy Larcom

On with the dance! Let joy be unconfined!

Lord Byron

Life is the flower for which love is the honey.

Victor Hugo

A friend is one who knows you
and loves you just the same.

Elbert Hubbard

best

friends

SWEET TREATS A FRIEND
LOVES TO HEAR:

❖ her best friend's laughter
❖ the ring of the phone
❖ the words "I care about you"

A little sweet cupcake
With fluffy pink icing;
So easy to bake
And perfect for slicing.

Yes, we must ever be friends; and of all who offer you friendship let me be ever the first, the truest, the nearest and dearest!

Henry Wadsworth Longfellow

You are as sweet as a double-scoop, chocolate-dipped, rainbow-sprinkled, strawberry ice-cream cone.

*Friendship is the
breathing rose,
with sweets in
every fold.*

Oliver Wendell Holmes

A good laugh is
sunshine in the house.

William Makepeace Thackeray

SWEET TREATS TO REVIVE
A WEARY FRIEND:

- ❖ a shoulder to lean on
- ❖ a hand to hold
- ❖ an understanding heart

SWEET TREATS TO BLESS A FRIEND:

- ❖ love
- ❖ loyalty
- ❖ prayers

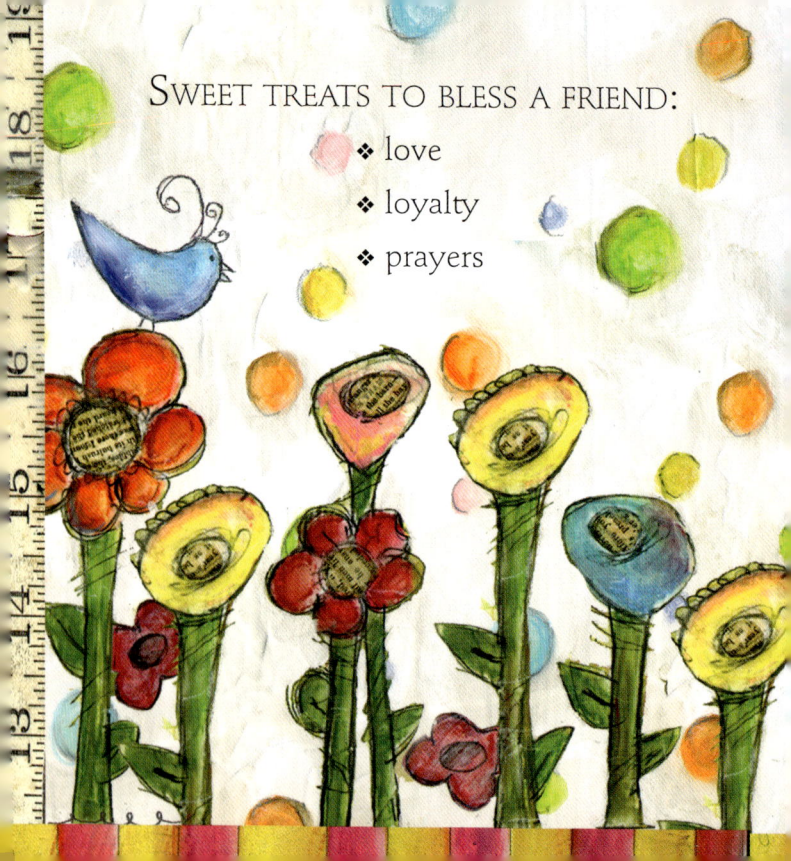

The sweet things in life—
girlfriends, giggles, grins,
and gumdrops!

Scatter joy.

Ralph Waldo Emerson

eat

cake

yum

Oh-So-Easy Cherry Cobbler

- 1 (15 ounce) can pitted tart red cherries, drained with liquid reserved
- ½ cup white sugar
- 1 cup buttermilk baking mix
- ½ cup white sugar
- ½ cup milk

Preheat oven to 350 degrees. Spray a 9x9 inch baking dish with cooking spray. Stir together the liquid from cherries and ½ cup sugar. Heat mixture 1–2 minutes in microwave until sugar is dissolved. Set aside. Mix baking mix, ½ cup sugar, and milk together in separate bowl to make a moist batter. Spread evenly in bottom of baking dish. Spread cherries evenly over the batter. Slowly pour the cherry juice over the cherries. Bake 25–30 minutes until lightly browned.

SWEET TREATS TO START A PERFECT DAY:

❖ delicious cinnamon scones

❖ hot brewed tea

❖ a long chat with a kindred spirit

Celebrate love. It is the breath of your existence and the best of all reasons for living.

Author Unknown

my

SWEET

treat

Heavenly Apple Dessert

- 1 (8 ounce) package cream cheese, softened
- ¼ cup white sugar
- ¾ cup caramel ice-cream topping
- 3 (1.4 ounce) bars chocolate-covered English toffee, chopped
- 5 green apples, cored and sliced

Mix together cream cheese, sugar, and ¼ cup caramel sauce. Spread mixture onto a serving tray. Drizzle remaining caramel sauce over the top and sprinkle with chopped candy pieces. Refrigerate for 30 minutes. Serve with apple slices.

Cupcakes + Friends = Bliss

FOR

ME

Gourmet Root Beer Float

- ½ pint vanilla ice cream
- 1 (12 ounce) can or bottle root beer
- ½ cup whipped cream
- 4 maraschino cherries

Place 1 scoop of ice cream into each of two tall glasses. Pour root beer carefully over the ice cream. Add another scoop and repeat. Top with whipped cream and cherries.

In the cookies of life, friends are the chocolate chips.

Author Unknown

He hath the substance of all bliss,
To whom a virtuous friend is given;
So sweet harmonious friendship is,
Add but eternity, you'll make it heaven.

John Norris

SWEET TREATS TO
REFRESH A FRIEND'S SOUL:

- ❖ a handwritten note
- ❖ homemade cookies
- ❖ an unexpected gift

SWEET TREATS TO FIX A BAD DAY:

- ❖ a quiet walk
- ❖ a chocolate truffle
- ❖ a bubble bath

Friendship! the precious gold of life
By age refined, yet ever new;
Tried in the crucible of time
It always rings of service true.

Friendship! the beauteous soul of life
Which gladdens youth and strengthens age;
May it our hearts and lives entwine
Together on life's fleeting page.

Joseph Shaylor

All love is sweet,
Given or returned.
Common as light is love,
And its familiar voice wearies not ever.
They who inspire it most are fortunate
As I am now; but those who feel it most
Are happier still.

Percy Bysshe Shelley

Sweets to the sweet.

William Shakespeare

P A R T Y

Pretzel Peanut Bark

- ◆ 18 (1 ounce) squares white chocolate
- ◆ 3 cups pretzel sticks, broken then measured
- ◆ 2 cups dry salted peanuts

Line a rimmed cookie sheet with waxed paper. Melt chocolate in glass dish in microwave on high for 2 or more minutes, stirring at 1-minute intervals. Stir in pretzel pieces and peanuts. Spoon onto prepared cookie sheet and spread evenly. Cool, then break apart.

There is nothing on this earth more to be prized than true friendship.

Saint Thomas Aquinas

You are my
special treat...a
cherished friend so
lovely and true.

SWEET TREATS TO BRIGHTEN
A RAINY AFTERNOON:

❖ a gathering of friends

❖ fragrant, colorful bouquets of flowers

❖ a lifetime of memories

SWEET TREATS TO WARM MY FRIEND'S HEART:

- ❖ shared joy
- ❖ shared adventures
- ❖ shared comfort

Joy delights in joy.

William Shakespeare

let's eat

ICE CREAM

A *friend* is a present
you give yourself.

Robert Louis Stevenson

Cheers to you, my friend!

Joy is not in things;
it is in us.

Richard Wagner

CELEBRATE

Strawberry Angel Food Dessert

- 1 (10 inch) angel food cake
- 2 (8 ounce) packages cream cheese, softened
- 1 cup white sugar
- 1 (8 ounce) container frozen whipped topping, thawed
- 1 quart fresh strawberries, sliced
- 1 (18 ounce) jar strawberry glaze

Crumble the cake and mash it tightly into the bottom of a 9x13 inch baking dish. Beat the cream cheese and sugar in a medium bowl until light and fluffy. Fold in whipped topping. Spread mixture over cake. Combine strawberries and glaze until evenly coated. Spread over cream cheese layer. Chill well before serving.

A true friend reaches for your hand and touches your heart.

Author Unknown

No. XLI.

29

A true friend is a forever friend.

George MacDonald

A joy shared is a joy doubled.

Johann Wolfgang Von Goethe

And yet your fair discourse hath been as sugar, Making the hard way sweet and delectable.

William Shakespeare

Sugar and spice whip up nice!

*How rare and wonderful
is that flash of a moment
when we realize we have
discovered a friend.*

William E. Rothschild

We see things eye-to-eye and
feel things heart-to-heart.
You are my sweet friend.

You take the cake!

eat

CAKE

Éclair Cake

- 2 (3.5 ounce) packages instant vanilla pudding mix
- 1 (8 ounce) container frozen whipped topping, thawed
- 3 cups milk
- 1 (16 ounce) package graham cracker squares
- 1 (16 ounce) package prepared chocolate frosting

Thoroughly blend pudding mix, whipped topping, and milk. Arrange a single layer of graham cracker squares in 13x9 inch baking pan. Spread half of the pudding mixture over the crackers. Top with another layer of crackers and the remaining pudding mixture. Top with a final layer of crackers. Cover and chill for 30 minutes. Spread frosting over cake and chill at least 4 hours before serving.

Our friendship is sweeter than all the treats in the whole wide world!

Every time I think of you, I give thanks to my God. **The Book of Philippians**

all
to
herself

I thank my God for you.

Hold a true friend with
both your hands.

Nigerian Proverb

A friend is what the
heart needs all the time.

Henry Van Dyke